A Robbie Reader

THREAT TO ANCIENT EGYPTIAN TREASURES

Jim Whiting

Mitchell Lane
PUBLISHERS

P.O. Box 196
Hockessin, Delaware 19707
Visit us on the web: www.mitchelllane.com
Comments? email us: mitchelllane@mitchelllane.com

Mitchell Lane PUBLISHERS

Printing   4   5   6   7   8   9

A Robbie Reader/On the Verge of Extinction: Crisis in the Environment

Library of Congress Cataloging-in-Publication Data
Whiting, Jim, 1943–
    Threat to ancient Egyptian treasures / by Jim Whiting.
        p. cm. — (A Robbie reader. On the verge of extinction: crisis in the environment)
    Includes bibliographical references and index.
    ISBN 978-1-58415-588-1 (library bound)
    I. Egypt—Antiquities—Conservation and restoration—Juvenile literature. 2. Historic sites—Conservation and restoration—Egypt—Juvenile literature. I. Title.
DT60.W47 2007
932—dc22
                                                                    2007000817

ABOUT THE AUTHOR: Jim Whiting has been a remarkably versatile and accomplished journalist, writer, editor, and photographer for more than 30 years. He has a keen interest in the natural world. A voracious reader since early childhood, Mr. Whiting has written and edited more than 250 nonfiction children's books on a wide range of topics. He lives in Washington state with his wife and two teenage sons.

PHOTO CREDITS: Cover, pp. I, 3, 4, 7, 20, 22, 25—© 2008 JupiterImages Corporation; p. 10—Getty Images; p. 14—NASA.

TABLE OF CONTENTS

Words in **bold** type can be found in the glossary.

Rameses II, also known as Rameses the Great, was one of the most famous Egyptian rulers in ancient times. Rameses, who had a very high opinion of himself, had many monuments built to show the Egyptian people how great he was.

A MONUMENTAL EGO

Egypt is one of the oldest civilizations in the world. Its history reaches back more than 5,000 years. It is an important country for **archaeologists** (ar-kee-AH-luh-jists). Archaeologists study ancient civilizations to learn how people lived during those times.

For much of its history, Egypt was ruled by a **pharaoh** (FAH-roh), or king. One of the most famous pharaohs was Rameses (RAM-zeez) II. His rule began about 1279 BCE and lasted for more than 65 years. Historians call him Rameses the Great. By Egyptian standards, even his personal life was "great." He had dozens of wives and about 200 children.

Rameses thought very highly of himself. He built many monuments throughout Egypt that honored him. The most famous was Abu Simbel (AH-boo SIM-bell). It was carved out of solid rock on a steep hill that overlooks the Nile River, Egypt's most important waterway.

Four huge statues of Rameses are seated at the front of Abu Simbel. These statues are 70 feet high. More statues of Rameses are

Two of ancient Egypt's most important gods honor Rameses. Seth, the lord of Lower (northern) Egypt, is on the left. Horus, who represents Upper Egypt, stands to the right.

The waters of Lake Nasser lap on the shoreline just below the current location of Abu Simbel. The temple's original site has been underwater since the early 1960s.

inside. Rameses thought he was so important that he even included a statue of himself seated next to three gods that were worshiped by ancient Egyptians.

In the twentieth century, Abu Simbel became one of Egypt's most famous tourist attractions. Thousands of people visited it every year. They brought a lot of money into the country.

The statue of Rameses the Great inside the temple in Abu Simbel stands over 30 feet tall. The walls are covered with rows of carvings that explain some of Rameses' accomplishments.

In the early 1960s, the Egyptian government planned to build a large dam on the Nile River. Known as the Aswan Dam, it would provide electrical power and would **regulate** (REH-gyuh-layt) the amount of water that could be used for growing crops. However, the dam would create a huge lake, called Lake Nasser, that would put Abu Simbel under nearly 200 feet of water. The famous monument would be gone forever.

The Egyptians didn't want to lose the monument. They were very proud of what their **ancestors** (AN-ses-turs) had done, and Abu Simbel was a symbol of this pride in their history. People all over the world felt the same way, so they worked together to save it. First, they carefully **dismantled** the monument. Then they put it back together higher up the hill. This process took four years and cost millions of dollars, but the effort paid off. Tourists continue to flock to Abu Simbel. Its story, so far, has had a happy ending.

King Tutankhamen, better known as King Tut, was buried in a casket made of solid gold. The discovery of King Tut's burial site in 1922 made headlines around the world.

THE VALLEY OF THE KINGS

Egypt is full of ancient monuments such as Abu Simbel. Nearly all of them are in danger.

One of the most treasured monuments also involves Rameses II. When he died, his **mummified** (MUH-mih-fyd) body was laid to rest in the Valley of the Kings, a burial site for pharaohs. Many royal tombs are located there. Like Abu Simbel, the Valley of the Kings is next to the Nile River.

One of the most famous gravesites in the Valley of the Kings belonged to King Tutankhamen (too-tang-KAH-mun). Better known as King Tut, he was an **obscure** pharaoh who died more than 3,300 years ago.

He was still a teenager when he died. Some people believe that he was murdered.

Tutankhamen's body was buried in an **ornate** tomb. A huge stash of gold, jewels, and other valuable objects was buried along with him. The ancient Egyptians believed that he needed those objects in the **afterlife**.

One of the most impressive objects in King Tut's tomb is his casket, which is made of solid gold. Objects have been borrowed from the tomb and used for popular exhibitions that travel to museums all over the world.

Archaeologists continue to work in the Valley of the Kings and are still making important discoveries there. Early in 2006, they found a new tomb. They also found an ancient street that had been lined with a thousand stone **sphinxes** (SFINK-ses). They believe other treasures are in the valley, just waiting to be uncovered.

Meanwhile, the Valley of the Kings is in danger. For many centuries, robbers had been breaking into the gravesites, stealing many priceless pieces and causing a lot of damage to the tombs.

The area around the Valley of the Kings is subject to sudden heavy flooding. The Aswan Dam changed the flow of the Nile River. The water level has risen. New roads, which were made so that tourists could more easily reach the site, have increased **erosion** (eh-ROH-zhun). The erosion allows more water to collect near the valley. At least one tomb has been completely destroyed by the resulting floods. Others have been damaged.

Still another problem is that Egypt is one of the fastest-growing countries in the world. It must grow a lot of food to feed its people. The Aswan Dam has made more land available to farmers. Some of the new farmland is very close to the Valley of the Kings. The farmers often flood their fields to help their crops grow. This water can seep into the archaeological sites and damage them.

Queens' Pyramids

Menkaure

Sphinx

Valley Temple

Khafre

Queens' Pyramids

Khufu

Ancient Egyptian pyramids were royal tombs. Each is named for the king buried within. Egyptian queens were buried in smaller pyramids. Another treasure, the Great Sphinx, guards the pyramids of Giza.

THE PYRAMIDS

Before pharaohs were buried in the Valley of the Kings, some of them had pyramids built as their gravesites. Three of the most famous are located at Giza (GEE-zuh), just outside the Egyptian capital of Cairo (KY-roh). The largest, called the Great Pyramid, was constructed for a pharaoh named Khufu (KOO-foo).

The Great Pyramid is over 450 feet high. For more than 4,000 years, it was the tallest human-made structure on earth. It contains over two million individual stone blocks. Each block weighs more than two tons. No one knows exactly how these heavy stones were hauled up the sides of the pyramid.

The other two pyramids are almost as high as the Great Pyramid. They also served as burial sites for pharaohs who lived at about the same time as Khufu. All three of these pyramids are in danger.

Part of the problem is their popularity. People travel from all over the world to view the pyramids. When they walk inside the pyramids, their breath **condenses** and forms salt on the walls. Salt is very harmful to the stones. Some visitors even like to carve their names into the walls when no one is looking, adding to the damage.

The vast increase in the amount of transportation near the pyramids also endangers the monuments. Heavy trucks, millions of cars, and even airplanes flying overhead produce vibrations that can crack the ancient stones. These vehicles and other human activity generate pollution. The pollution slowly eats away at the stones.

Humans aren't the only enemy. Nature is also on the attack. The Great Pyramid was originally covered by a layer of smooth stone.

The Great Pyramid is one of the most famous human-made structures in the world. It has endured for more than 40 centuries.

Centuries of desert winds carrying sand have slowly eroded this layer. As a result, the Great Pyramid is 30 feet shorter today than when it was built.

Taken together, the three pyramids are considered one of the Seven Wonders of the Ancient World. They are the only one of the seven to survive into the present time. People want the pyramids to continue to survive, to remind us all of past greatness.

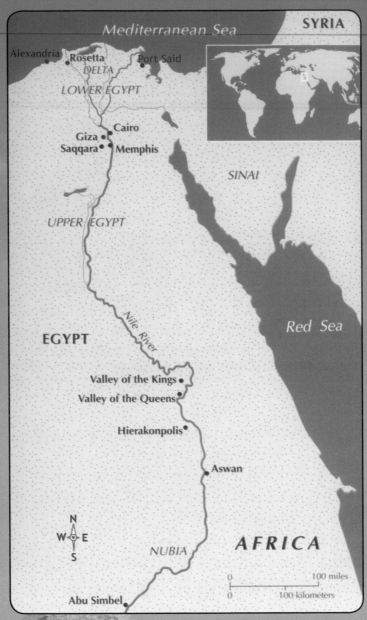

Many of Egypt's treasures are close to the Nile River, where people have lived for over 5,000 years. The river flows north through the country. It empties into the Mediterranean Sea.

OTHER IMPORTANT SITES IN DANGER

The Great Sphinx is another famous Egyptian monument. This massive stone **sculpture** (SKULP-chur) is also in Giza, very close to the pyramids. It has the head of a pharaoh and the body of a lion. Like the pyramids, the Sphinx has suffered from erosion and winds. Its nose disappeared many years ago. It also suffered when workers used cement to restore it in the 1980s. The cement didn't react well with the limestone that was used to build the original monument.

Another notable site is at Helwan, a town about fifteen miles south of Cairo. It is valuable to archaeologists because it gives

The Great Sphinx is 240 feet long. The top of the head rises nearly 70 feet above the desert. It has the body of a lion and the head of a pharaoh.

them ideas about how common people lived in ancient times. Meanwhile, the Egyptian army has a large base nearby, and new housing projects are being built steadily closer to where archaeologists are doing their work.

Hierakonpolis (hy-uh-ruh-KON-puh-lis) is one more site that has many treasures.

One of the most famous is the world's oldest mud hut. It has endured for more than 5,000 years, but it has become increasingly endangered. The Egyptian government has announced plans to relocate about 100,000 people from other parts of Egypt close to Hierakonpolis. Increased farming there brings water closer to the site, which can damage the objects that archaeologists study.

Meanwhile, some looting has taken place. The thieves sell what they have stolen, and the treasures disappear.

A number of lesser-known sites are located in the Nile Delta, where the Nile River splits into smaller branches. It is very close to sea level. As **global warming** continues, the sea continues to rise, and many of these sites can become flooded. Much of Egypt's increasing population lives in this already crowded area. As is the case with Helwan, new houses are often built dangerously close to archaeological sites.

EXTINCTION

Modern-day Cairo is one of the most densely populated—and one of the most polluted—cities in the world. More than 15 million people live there. Many high-rise buildings line the shores of the Nile River.

WHAT CAN BE DONE?

Ancient Egyptian treasures face more than one danger. Some of the dangers are natural, such as the sandstorms that sweep across the desert. Other dangers are clearly human caused, such as Egypt's skyrocketing population.

Just as in historical times, nearly everyone in Egypt lives near the Nile River. The rest of Egypt is desert, where it is far too hot and dry for people to live in permanent settlements. There simply isn't much room left anymore. More and more people are living near sites that were isolated just a few years earlier.

Air pollution is another problem. Harsh chemicals in the air eat away at the ancient stones. Global warming is also a factor. While most scientists believe that world temperature increases are caused by human activity, some disagree. But there is no doubt that the earth has become warmer in recent decades.

Almost everyone agrees that saving these ancient sites is important. Not long ago, the Egyptian government changed the location of a highway that would have passed very close to the pyramids. In a few cases, villages that were next to important sites have been moved farther away. But, despite its best efforts, the government can't afford the enormous amount of money it will take to save the sites. Does that mean that the situation is hopeless?

While no one knows what the future will bring, there are some encouraging signs. A group of well-known Egyptian archaeologists founded the Egyptian Cultural Heritage Organization, or ECHO. Its purpose is to make more people aware that saving Egypt's ancient treasures is important, and to raise money to help save them. Other private groups have the same goals.

The people of Egypt aren't alone. People all over the world want to help. The United Nations Educational, Scientific and Cultural Organization (UNESCO) was responsible for collecting most of the money to save Abu Simbel. More than 50 countries participated. In 1972, UNESCO established the World

Pharaoh Djoser built the Step Pyramid around 2650 BCE. It stands about 180 feet high. It is near modern-day Cairo.

Heritage Center. The center's goal is to preserve important historical and cultural sites around the world. Many of these sites are in Egypt.

Another international group that is focusing on saving historical treasures is the World Monuments Watch, organized by the World Monuments Fund. The Watch looks for monuments that are in particular danger, then offers to send experts and money to try to solve the problem. Egypt has received assistance from this group.

There's no doubt that the pyramids and Egypt's other ancient wonders are worth saving. Let's hope their stories have the same happy ending as Abu Simbel.

The Great Pyramid, Giza

Learn About Ancient Egypt

Ancient Egypt is a very interesting place and time to study. Find out why its treasures are so valuable, then help spread the word of how these important sites are in danger. For example, you can find out how and why the ancient Egyptians made mummies. Some books contain fun projects that you can easily do.

Share what you learn with your family, friends, and classmates. The more people who value these treasures, the more likely it is that something will be done to preserve them.

Work for a Greener Earth

Any time you can save energy (such as turning off lights when you're not using them) or resources (such as recycling trash and not letting the water run while you brush your teeth), you are helping the environment.

Join a Conservation Organization

You can join an organization that is working to save Egyptian treasures. For example, student membership in the Egyptian Cultural Heritage Organisation (ECHO) is relatively inexpensive. Their website is http://www.e-c-h-o.org/.

Respect the Treasures of the World

If you are lucky enough to be able to visit some of the sites mentioned in this book, be sure not to touch them or do anything else that might cause damage. Avoid the temptation to keep a piece of treasure for yourself. Stay on established pathways, and be sure not to litter.

TIMELINE

NOTE: While many scholars accept the following timeline, there is not unanimous agreement, and some sources indicate alternate dates.

BCE

3300	Approximate time that writing began in Egypt.
2686	The reign of Djoser, who built the Step Pyramid, begins.
2589	The reign of Khufu, who built the Great Pyramid at Giza, begins.
1539	Burials begin in the Valley of the Kings.
1334	Tutankhamen (King Tut) becomes pharaoh.
1325	Tutankhamen dies under mysterious circumstances and is buried in the Valley of the Kings.
1304	Probable date of birth of Rameses II.
1279	Rameses II becomes pharaoh.
1269	Rameses II begins building Abu Simbel.
1256	Abu Simbel is dedicated.
1212	Rameses II dies.
1075	Burials end in the Valley of the Kings.

CE

1743	Richard Pococke draws first modern map of the Valley of the Kings.
1813	Swiss explorer J. L. Burckhardt rediscovers Abu Simbel after it has been buried by sand for many centuries.
1822	French scholar Jean François Champollion deciphers the Rosetta Stone, which allows people to read ancient Egyptian writing.
1922	Archaeologist Howard Carter discovers the tomb of King Tut.
1965	World Monuments Fund is founded.
1968	Abu Simbel opens on its new site.
1970	Aswan Dam is completed, creating the huge Lake Nasser.
1972	The United Nations creates the World Heritage Center.
1995	The World Monuments Fund institutes World Monuments Watch.
2006	American archaeologists discover a new tomb in the Valley of the Kings.
2007	Egyptian President Hosni Mubarak officially opens the Mubarak Historical Centre in Luxor, where one third of Egypt's monuments are located.

Books

Beilenson, Suzanne, and Martha Day Zschock. *Ancient Egypt Scratch & Sketch: An Art Activity Book for Inquisitive Artists and Archaeologists of All Ages.* Mount Vernon, New York: Peter Pauper Press, 2006.

Donnelly, Judy. *Tut's Mummy: Lost . . . and Found.* New York: Random House, 1988.

Gibbons, Gail. *Mummies, Pyramids, and Pharaohs: A Book About Ancient Egypt.* New York: Little, Brown, 2004.

Logan, Claudia. *The 5,000-Year-Old Puzzle: Solving a Mystery of Ancient Egypt.* New York: Farrar, Straus and Giroux, 2002.

Reynolds, Jeff. *Egypt: A to Z.* Danbury, Connecticut: Children's Press, 2005.

Ross, Stewart. *Egypt in Spectacular Cross-Section.* New York: Scholastic, 2005.

Sands, Emily, Nick Harris, et. al. *Egyptology.* Cambridge, Massachusetts: Candlewick Press, 2004.

Steele, Philip. *Curious Kids Guides: Ancient Egypt.* New York: Kingfisher, 2002.

Tagholm, Sally. *Ancient Egypt: A Guide to Egypt in the Time of the Pharaohs.* New York: Kingfisher, 1999.

Works Consulted

ABC News Online: "Valley of the Kings Tomb Uncovered"
http://www.abc.net.au/news/newsitems/200602/s1567544.htm

Archaeology: "Insight: The World's Most Endangered Sites"
http://www.archaeology.org/9911/etc/insight.html

BBC: *Ancient History: Egyptians*
http://www.bbc.co.uk/history/ancient/egyptians

Carnegie Museum of Natural History: *Life in Ancient Egypt*
http://www.carnegiemnh.org/exhibits/egypt/index.htm

Cerveny, Randy, and Niccole Cerveny. "Egypt and Water: The Lifeline of a Civilization."
http://www.weatherwise.org/feafull.php

Clayton, Peter A. *Chronicles of the Pharaohs*. London: Thames & Hudson, 1994.

Crystalinks: *Valley of the Kings*
http://www.crystalinks.com/valleykings.html

Egyptian Cultural Heritage Organization
http://www.e-c-h-o.org/background.htm

Hobson, Christine. *The World of the Pharaohs: A Complete Guide to Ancient Egypt.* London: Thames & Hudson, 1987.

Menu, Bernadette. *Ramesses II: Greatest of the Pharaohs.* New York: Harry N. Abrams, 1999.

Odyssey Online: Egypt
http://carlos.emory.edu/odyssey/egypt/homepg.html

The Seven Wonders: The Great Pyramid of Giza
http://ce.eng.usf.edu/pharos/wonders/pyramid.html

Web Addresses

Ancient Egypt
http://www.ancientegypt.co.uk

Explore the Pyramids—NOVA Online
http://www.pbs.org/wgbh/nova/pyramid/explore

Guardian's Egypt: *Ancient Egypt*
http://guardians.net/egypt

History for Kids: *Ancient Egypt*
http://www.historyforkids.org/learn/egypt/index.htm

Tour Egypt for Kids: *Color Me Egypt*
http://www.touregypt.net/kids/

GLOSSARY

afterlife (AF-tur-lyf)—in ancient Egyptian belief, an existence in some form after death.

ancestors (AN-ses-turs)—people in the past who are related to a person or group of people.

archaeologist (ar-kee-AH-luh-jist)—a scientist who studies ancient peoples and how they lived.

condenses (kun-DEN-ses)—turns from a gas form into a liquid form.

dismantled (dis-MAN-tuld)—took apart carefully.

erosion (eh-ROH-zhun)—slowly wearing away, often as a result of water or wind.

global warming—an overall warming of the earth as a result of human activity.

mummified (MUH-mih-fyd)—made into a mummy by removing internal organs and drying the body.

obscure (ob-SKYOOR)—not well known; not seen very clearly.

ornate (or-NAYT)—highly decorated or fancy.

pharaoh (FAH-roh)—an Egyptian king.

regulate (REH-gyuh-layt)—to adjust the rate at which something happens.

sculpture (SKULP-chur)—three-dimensional art made of wood, stone, or other solid material.

sphinx (SFINKS)—an ancient Egyptian image with the body of a lion lying down and the head of either a man, a ram, or a hawk. The Great Sphinx has the head of a pharaoh.